THEN AND NOW

The Changing Scene
of
Surrey Village Life
in
BANSTEAD

a publication by

The Banstead History Research Group

The cover photograph is The Old Well, Park Road,
Banstead in 1908. The children in the picture are from the right,
Rose Harbour, Annie Birt, Emily Farley, Dolly Crawley, Gladys Hicks
and Maggie Muggeridge, together with an unknown insurance man.

First Edition October 1987
Reprint with supplement October 1998
© Banstead History Research Group
All rights reserved. No reproduction
permitted by any means without the
express permission in writing of
the Publishers
Banstead History Research Group

ISBN 0 9512741 4 7

Printed by Denyer Printers, Lower Road,
Kenley, Surrey CR8 5NH

Acknowledgements

Production. This was by a sub-committee of the Banstead History Research Group comprising J.I. Hay, P.D. Hodson, D. Johnson, R. Packham and B.A. Rough who were assisted by M. Cory, P. Mason and I. O'Shea.

New Photographs. These were taken mainly by G. Davies assisted by E. Dansey, D. Gilham, M. Hay, G. Johnson and L. Pruce. The final prints were produced with the help of Banstead Photographic. Our thanks are expressed to those residents of Banstead who permitted our photographers to enter their property to take pictures.

Old Photographs. These are mainly from the collections of the BHRG, P.D. Hodson and R. Packham but we are grateful to the following who kindly permitted us to reproduce their photographs or documents:
L. Bond, M. Crook, W. Gordon, M. Grigsby, G.K. Kempsell, J. Lacey, J. Marshall, G. Pushman, B. Shivas, Banstead Central Library, Banstead Cricket Club and Surrey County Council.

Donations & Loans. Generous help was given by the following people and organisations which enabled us to finance this project:
Banstead Community Association, J. Clifford Esq., Confederation of Health Service Employees, Federated Pension Schemes, W.A. Hutchinson Esq., Legal & General Assurance Society Ltd., Messrs. A. & E. Longhurst, H. Page Esq., Workers Educational Association. Without their help this book could not have been published.

Publicity. The following four organisations gave invaluable assistance to us by enabling our Advance Order Form to be included in their distributed bulletins:
Banstead Arts Festival Society, Banstead Community Association, Nork Residents & Ratepayers Association, Workers Educational Association. Our thanks go to all the Road Stewards who, as a result, carried more paper on their rounds.

It is inevitable that in a publication such as this some mistakes will be found in the text. For this we apologise and we would welcome comments from our readers together with any additional information they can contribute.

Introduction to 1998 version

The photographs and text of the original edition have been reproduced without amendment. To show some major changes since 1987 - eg demolition of the old Village School - a supplement has been added. This contains new photographs and captions referring back to the original edition and numbered accordingly. Where this has been done, the relevant pages in the original edition have been marked with an asterisk.

Source Data

Many sources were referred to and we were helped by the memories and reminiscences of past and present residents of the district. The following texts are recommended for further study:

Lambert H.C.M.	History of Banstead in Surrey Vol. I (1912) & Vol. II (1930) OUP
O'Shea I.	Village School, Banstead (1981) BHRG
Randall V.	Focus on Banstead: Reminiscences of a local moviemaker (1971)
Kirkby J.R.W.	The Banstead & Epsom Downs Railway (1983) The Oakwood Press
BHRG	Banstead - A History (1993)

Preface

This book has been produced by the Banstead History Research Group which began in 1974 as a result of W.E.A. lectures given by Mr. Ronald Michell. He very skilfully provided the initial impetus to the group and then withdrew, almost without us noticing.

There are now twenty members. We undertake research projects, mount exhibitions, provide lectures, attempt to conserve the little that is left of old Banstead as well as building up an archive of photographs, documents and data relating to this area.

It is therefore fitting that we dedicate this book to Ron Michell, an ardent local historian.

Introduction

From Neolithic settlement to Regency grandeur, Victorian prosperity to inter-war urban development; despite Banstead's long existence it is not easy for anyone to learn about its history. We hope that this book will go some way towards filling this gap. The pictures and photographs give tantalising glimpses of Banstead's past, though the record is far from being complete. Lack of space in this volume has made some gaps inevitable. In other cases we have not traced old illustrations and would be delighted to know of any we could copy for the archives.

There is as yet only a little evidence of early life in this area, like a cache of iron, probably left by an itinerant smith, on the Downs near the hospital. However, our Saxon ancestors lived and died here as we know from the skeletons and grave goods which have been excavated.

We find more positive documentation in the Domesday Book when Benestede – the place where beans grow – was recorded as a village with a church whose overlord was William the Conqueror's brother, Odo, Bishop of Bayeux. The man who is arguably our most notable resident, Hubert de Burgh, Justiciar to King John, was the Lord of the Manor and his name lives on around us in various guises. The popularity of hunting brought at least three medieval kings to pursue this sport in Banstead Park, now Banstead Woods. They stayed in the Manor House near to All Saints Church, which later was part of Catherine of Aragon's dowry. Sadly the house disappeared leaving its exact whereabouts a mystery.

For many generations Banstead was a small agricultural community centred around the Well, its people working the open fields which stretched northwards from the High Street. Sheep grazed on the chalk Downs, whose herbage imparted such a good flavour to the meat that Banstead mutton became famous.

In the 18th century large houses were built, some by local families like the Buckles and the Lamberts, others as country residences for the wealthy. Establishments such as Nork House, Garratts Hall, Banstead Place, Rooks Nest and Yewlands provided additional employment for the villagers who numbered about 700 at the beginning of the 19th century.

The improvements in road travel and the coming of the railway had a gradual impact on Banstead by making it more accessible to London and the 1920s onwards saw a transformation of the district. Thousands of 'desirable residences' were erected as the large estates were sold off. However, Banstead still retains some of its village qualities; the Well remains though the ponds in the High Street have been filled in; the medieval spire of All Saints presides over the High Street surrounded by its churchyard, an oasis of green.

It is unfortunate that the flying bomb which fell in 1944 destroyed the nucleus of the old village and that, after the war, the need for modern housing and faster transport has over-ruled conservation. So, considering the age of the settlement, there are now surprisingly few pre 20th century buildings in Banstead. We realise that some change is inevitable but a judicious blending of old and new in our surroundings adds variety to life. Therefore we hope you enjoy this book and that it will encourage everyone to guard our heritage for future generations.

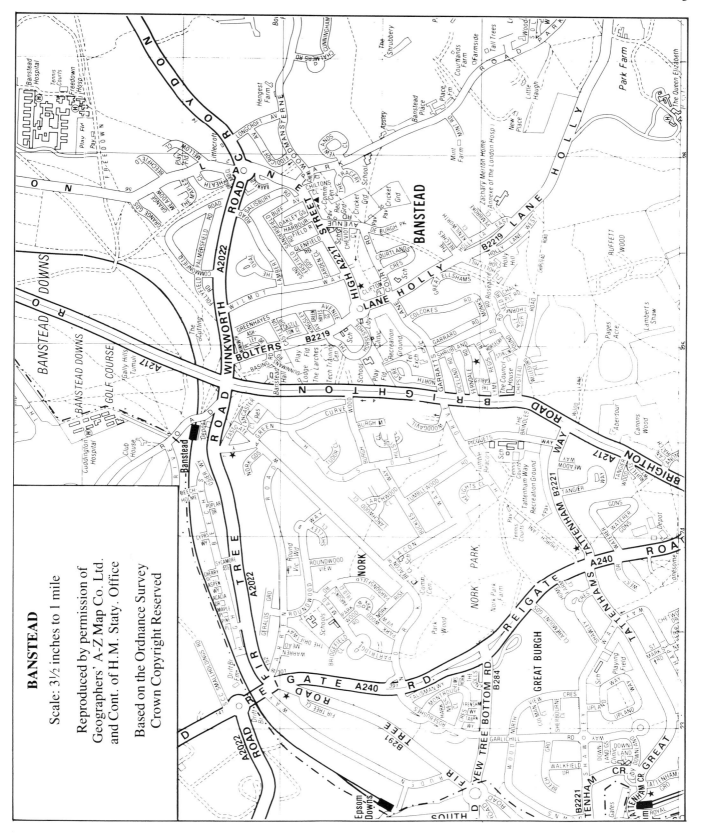

The Victoria Hotel, Banstead

The Victoria Public House was built about 1864 using chalk from the newly dug railway cuttings as foundations. The old hoarding advertised 'Fine Ales, Stout & Porter' brewed by Hodgsons of Kingston who were later incorporated into Courage & Co.. In 1867 Richard Payne was the landlord but from about 1870 to the 1930s the Gilbert family ran the pub. Tom Gilbert, whose name appears over the door, was Captain of the Cricket Club and also a farmer. The vine in the greenhouse is over 100 years old.

Bolters Pond, also known as Gilbert's Pond, was across the road until 1929. There was a way in and out for the horses and carts and it is rumoured that once the policeman's horse became stuck in the mud, much to the amusement of the local lads!

Winkworth Cottage was over 300 years old when it was removed in 1937, some say to be rebuilt in America. It had been part of Winkworth Farm. In more recent times the cottage was a popular tea room, famous for its cream teas and the bread oven by the side of the fireplace in the tea lounge. It was set back from the High Street at the end of the alleyway now at the side of Cullens. Greenhayes Avenue can be seen in the top left of the old postcard and Wilmot Way to the right.

OUR CELEBRATED DEVONSHIRE TEAS (Ad lib)

Home-Made Rolls and Girdle Cakes with Jam and Cream,
Assorted Cakes   ::   ::   Is. 6d. per person
            Without Cream   Is. 3d. per person.
            Without Cream and Jam Is. per person.
Notice—   On Week Ends and Bank Holidays only set teas
will be served.

TARIFF

Coffee, per cup	4d.	Tea, China or Indian,	
Milk, hot or cold,		per pot per person	4d.
per glass	3d.	Roll or Scone and	
Lemonade or Orangeade,		Butter, each	2d.
per glass	4d.	Bread and Butter,	
Cakes (various), each	2d.	per portion	2d.

Cream Ices 3d., 6d., 9d. and Is.

The Lounge is open for Morning Coffees and Afternoon Teas
from Easter until September 30th (Mondays excepted).

All Saints - Ch. Banstead.

All Saints Church is the oldest building in Banstead. A church was on this site in the time of Domesday but the oldest parts of the present structure date from about 1200. Over the years the church has undergone many additions and alterations, in particular in 1716 and again in the 1860s. From the south east corner of the graveyard the oldest grave is just visible. Covered in ivy in front of the West window is the large tomb of John Ludlow, citizen of London buried in 1722. Also here are the graves of Allen Sarle, Henry Knibbs and many members of the Lambert and Buckle families. There are several 18th century headstones remaining giving us the names of some of the families who lived here then – Woodman, Muggeridge and Page. Two of the chest tombs are listed Grade II.

The picture of the Christmas decorations showing the wall paintings inside the church is from a card postmarked 1911. Of these, only the painting of Christ on the cross remains today. Many years before, probably during Oliver Cromwell's time, a mural was removed from the church to Well Farm for safekeeping as it said 'Fear God and Honour the King'. The font on the right is 14th century.

BANSTEAD VICARAGE

The Vicarage, situated where Woolworth's is now, was the only building in this part of the High Street between the church and Bolters Lane. John Aubrey writing in the 17th century described it as having a fine collection of laurels, ivy and hollies. In 1824 it was considerably enlarged. From 1823 to 1905 three members of the Buckle family, grandfather, father and son, were vicars. Part of the land was sold in 1933 for the new Crown Post Office and planning permission was given in 1937 for a cinema on the site of the Vicarage. The Vicarage itself was sold in 1937 and a new one built in Garratts Lane, which was recently replaced in 1973 by the one in Court Road.

MARCH, 1905.

THE

All Saints, Banstead
PARISH MAGAZINE.

In Memoriam.

EDWARD VALENTINE BUCKLE, M.A.

CURATE, 1857—1865.   VICAR from 1865—1905.

REQUIESCAT IN PACE.

Entrance to Banstead Church.   6267. B Bros.

The trees which flank the entrance to the Church were there when this old postcard was taken, but opposite the open fields stretched to the Downs. The orchard in front of the Church is now a welcome open space in a busy shopping street.

The Church Institute was built in 1906 at the instigation of the Vicar and paid for by his brother. Part of the Orchard was taken as building land. One resident remembers seeing a lantern slide show, given by Miss Acland, of places she had visited around the world. Other entertainments at the Institute were the BI Minstrels and concerts. It was used once a week pre-war as Banstead's first public Library and for the Infant Welfare Clinic.

On this occasion our intrepid photographer stood in the centre of the road to take the comparable new picture. This is not often possible but it does show how much the road has been widened.

These two elegant villas dated from the mid 19th century. The one next to the Institute was the home of the verger Jeffrey Shove, hence the path next to the Institute became Shove's Path. Next door the house was called 'Tuffleigh'; in 1927 Mr. Robertson the dentist was here and later Lewis & Son, veterinary surgeons. The houses were demolished in 1962 to make way for the row of shops.

The Pond circa 1913

Brew Bros 1979

Commercial Development 1987

The pond was drained in 1929 to take the petrol tanks for French & Foxwell's, later Brew's, garage and the ducks had to find a new home. The garage was demolished in 1983 but the tree survives with the help of a preservation order. The tree and the garage can be seen on the right in the picture above. The shops were built in the early 1930s on part of the Buff House estate. On the left are older shops including a tea room and in the far distance is Watkin's garage. The ice cream tricycle is advertising, 'Large Bricks 1/6, Tubs 4d', an early 'Stop Me & Buy One' in the days before home freezers.

The postcard carries a date of 1931 and shows the shops of J. Taylor, newsagents, where the schoolchildren used to buy sweets, Wessons Fishmongers, and Smiths ironmongery, previously Balchins. Just beyond can be seen the View Cafe Refreshment Rooms which belonged to Mr. Townsend in 1927. This is the same cafe that appears in the foreground of the picture on page 15. The white house in the distance is the same in the old and new views. The shops were knocked down in 1962 to make way for new shops.

This house is something of a mystery! It stood on land which is now part of the school playground. The card is dated 1913; there is no bank on the corner but the school looks much the same now as then.

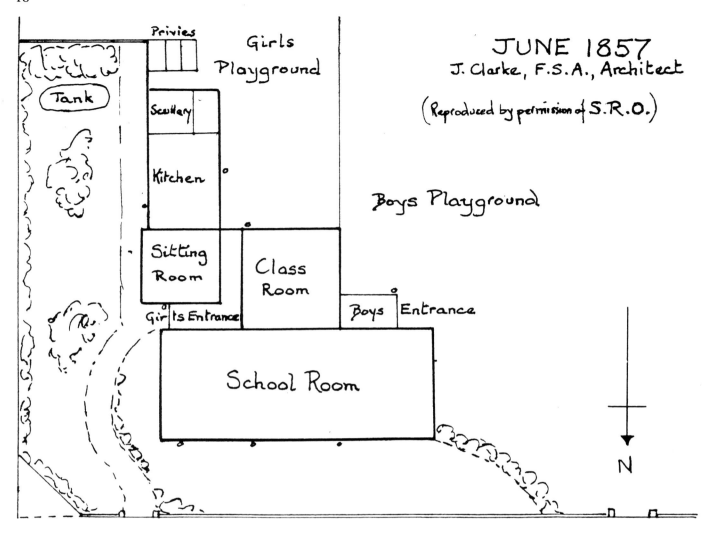

Privies

Girls Playground

Tank

Scullery

Kitchen

Sitting Room

Girls Entrance

Class Room

Boys Playground

Boys Entrance

School Room

JUNE 1857
J. Clarke, F.S.A., Architect

(Reproduced by permission of S.R.O.)

N

The Banstead Boys National School began in 1852 in a room opposite the Woolpack. Shortly afterwards it was felt necessary to build something more permanent; a piece of land was given by John Lambert and the present village school was begun. When it was opened in 1858 it looked like the drawing opposite. As the plan shows there was a main schoolroom fronting onto the High Street, just the three central windows of today's school, between the projecting gables.

The schoolmaster from 1862 to 1904 was Henry Knibbs. He is top left in the photograph. The other staff in 1902 were, from left to right; Back: Unknown, Nellie Moore, Unknown, H. Blackford, Daisy Muskett
Sitting: Harriet Knibbs, Jessie Norrington, Clara Balchin, Isabel Knibbs
Front: Wilfred Titterington, Grace Bennett, Evelyn Orton.

The Schools, Banstead.

THURSDAY, 21ST JANUARY, 1875.

A MUSICAL ENTERTAINMENT BY GEORGE BUCKLAND, ESQ. "GOSSIP AND SONG."

PART I.

INTRODUCTION—A few words about "Gossips" in general, Song writers and Song renderers.

DESCRIPTIVE SCENA, "The Maniac," *Russell.*

Music hath charms (under certain circumstances)—Its irritating and soothing properties—Music in the Workshop and in the Cottage.

DOMESTIC BALLAD, "Our Nell, or singing like a Bird," *G. Buckland.*

BALLADS OF THE NURSERY, "Spare the Rod and spoil the Child."

DOLEFUL SONG, "The naughty little Boy."
Written by *F. W. Green.* Music by *R. Coots.*

Our Journey due north.
SONG, "The Sleigh Drive," *Russell.*

The Silent Highway—The Sea in fiction, and the Sea in reality.

AQUATIC SKETCH, "A trip to the Nore," *J. W. Roe and G. Buckland.*

PART II.

Dramatic expressions. Varied melody required for changes of feeling.
SCENA, "Excelsior," *Blockley.*

Two sides to a question—A bit of Village Gossip.
HUMOROUS SONG, "Tittle Tattle," *G. Buckland.*

Music in the wind.
RECIT. AND AIR, "The Angel's Call," *Words by Tennyson.*

A new Tale of a Tub.
SMALL SONG, "Little Mr. Binks," *H. Walker.*

A moving Melodrama, in Three Acts, entitled

MADELINE MOMBRAY, THE MALTREATED MAIDEN,
OR
VILLANY VANQUISHED AND VIRTUE VICTORIOUS.

Banstead School.

At the side of the school a house was built for the schoolmaster. It is now used for the caretaker and as a staffroom. In 1895 the premises were enlarged and improved and again in 1906 when a separate Infants School began. The school building was used for entertainment for the village. The extract opposite is from the Winter 1874/5 programme. There are plans to build a new school in the Horseshoe and for this site to be used for other purposes. If this happens there will be only four buildings remaining in Banstead High Street which pre-date the 20th century.

The London & Provincial Bank first opened in 1905 in a wooden hut further down the High Street, (page 34). On Tuesday and Friday, Mr. Frank Wilton used to travel from Sutton in a horse drawn vehicle bringing cash with him. Sometimes he ran out and had to borrow from the landlord of the Woolpack. The bank moved to this site about 1911 and it became Barclays Bank in 1919. During rebuilding in 1969 it was housed in the new cricket pavilion.

High ST. Banstead. 2

Taken about 1910, Ortons Stores stood where Ricambio is today and Cunnington the butcher occupied the shop next door, now Amtool Hire. The butcher installed tile panels in the doorway depicting a calf and a lamb; the lamb is still there. The shop later became Parkers who moved from the corner of Sutton Lane to this site.

Buff House (above) stood at right angles to the High Street from where only the stable block was visible. It was built around 1800. The land belonging to the house stretched from opposite the Institute to opposite Ivy House and as far north as Banstead Downs and the railway.

From 1852 part of Buff House was used as a police station, the white building shown top right. In 1902 land was purchased from Mr. Lambert at a cost of £250 and a new police station was erected, opening on 23 July 1906. There was always a large force of men stationed here.

High Street, Bansted

This unusual view was taken in 1906 from the scaffolding during the construction of the new police station. The present station sergeant kindly let our photographer take the new view from a similar vantage point. At Ivy House, next door, is the sign of Alfred Dancy, plumber. For many years a transport business was operated from here. In 1911 Peter Coomber offered 'Open & Closed Carriages for Hire, Brakes etc. Est. 1898. Motors for Hire'. This became French & Foxwell's garage before they moved up the High Street. In the garden of Ivy House is a hand pump on a well. Piped water came to Banstead High Street about 1878 but many people preferred to keep their existing water supply rather than pay for the new one.

Buff Avenue was built on the eastern edge of the Buff House estate. The houses in the picture opposite which have the double gable mark the corner of the new road. Taken in 1933, this card shows the road before street lights had been installed. In 1930 the Parish Council minutes record that "there was no necessity or demand for street lighting of any kind within the Parish of Banstead".

Banstead Village.

Post Office, Banstead.

Banstead Village. (3)

Tonge's
Post Office Series. 566

GROCER &
PROVISION
MERCHANT.

B. A. TONGE,
Post Office Stores
BANSTEAD.

Families waited upon
daily for orders.
——
ESTABLISHED OVER 50 YEARS.

In 1839 John Cooper a builder who lived near the Woolpack, probably at Ivy House, received the letterpost daily at 12 noon and despatched it at 4.30pm. About 1855 a grocer's shop opened next door run by James Selsby. The Penny Post had begun in 1840 and Mr. Selsby became Postmaster. There were two deliveries of letters each day in 1871 and this increased to four by 1911. Helping in the shop in 1870 was James Tonge, his nephew. By 1890 Mr. Tonge had taken over the running of the shop to be followed by Mrs. Betsy Ann Tonge and from 1925, Mr. William Tonge. The bottom postcard has a sign indicating the public telephone in Tonge's; this began about 1910 and their number was Burgh Heath 10. In 1933 the Post Office moved temporarily to Turner's grocery in Buff Parade and the new Crown Post Office was opened in 1934.

There has been an inn on this site since earliest times. It first appears as the Woolpack in 1715 in church records as the parish business was conducted here. John Ingram was landlord in 1765; he also acted as barber for John Lambert of Well Farm and kept him supplied with wigs. For twenty years from the beginning of this century Samuel Stevens was landlord and then the Putnams.

THE WOOLPACK INN,

BANSTEAD,

Two-and-a-half Miles from Sutton Station.

EVERY ACCOMMODATION FOR LARGE AND SMALL PARTIES.

CLEAN & COMFORTABLE BEDROOMS.

Large Gardens neatly laid out.

Extensive Stabling & Lock-up Coach Houses.

·1860

This shows the eastern end of the village, the Woolpack is on the extreme right and the corner of the old bank is just beyond. At the beginning of this century on Derby Day, racegoers dressed up in old time costume and rode in brakes up Sutton Lane playing the Post Horn Gallop. They returned afterwards for drinks at the Woolpack. In the far distance the wall of Well House garden can be seen with two greenhouses behind. This whole area was devastated by the flying bomb in 1944.

The steps from the Woolpack came directly onto the road and it is said that by one of them was a metal strip indicating the height of St. Paul's Cathedral dome. The sign indicated that the brewery at the time was the Dartford brewery but it seems it changed from time to time. Prior to the establishment of a sub-post office in Banstead the Woolpack was the receiving house for the mail.

The cottages across the road were brick built with wood fronts. The shop at one time was Durlings sweet shop.

In this picture of the forge is Jack Shaw who was the last blacksmith. Before him the Palmers had been blacksmiths for over 60 years. The Shaws mainly did ironwork but they also shoed the horses for the Nork riding stables and the Garratts riding school. The activities of the smith and the warmth of the fire attracted many onlookers. The forge was another victim of the flying bomb. At that moment Mrs. Shaw was standing in the doorway with her husband talking to the sweep. They survived the event but the forge ended its days.

34

BANSTEAD VILLAGE.

Banstead

The Memorial, Banstead.

In the top picture opposite are a coffee room, later Ye Olde Tea Rooms, the first bank and the Woolpack. In 1839 horse drawn coaches left here daily for London. Motor bus services began in the 1920s; this one is going to Kingston.

The tall Corner House Tea Rooms (above) catered for walkers and the many cyclists enjoying a day out from London.

Many of the postcards shown in this book were sent by them as well as by people holidaying in Banstead. The round AA plaque gave useful mileages to weary travellers.

The signpost (see page 37) was replaced by the War Memorial, unveiled in 1921. Contrary to rumour it has never been moved, nor has it sunk but the road layout has changed.

Once called the Alley, Salisbury Road is almost as old as the High Street. By 1866 the gabled houses had replaced the original artisans cottages. In 1929 residents complained about the deplorable state of the road and of the noisy lorries going to the developing Buff House estate.

From 1871 to 1907 John Songhurst, bootmaker, occupied the left hand shop shown on page 37 which became Hodges Dairy. There was a butcher's shop on the corner of Sutton Lane in 1839 with a slaughterhouse behind. Henry Haydon worked there from 1862 and Henry Parker from 1918 until he moved (see page 23). Then Hodges Dairy took over.

Buses had difficulty negotiating the tight corner – on one occasion a window was shattered by an overhanging tree in the garden of Well House, on the right.

Circa 1905

Circa 1921

The Old Well, Banstead.

Tonges
Post Office Series

Well House was on the corner of Park Road and Woodmansterne Lane. It was built about 1650 and in 1680 the Killick family lived there. Sir Daniel Lambert bought the house in 1739 and it was the home of the Lamberts until the 20th century. The garden faced north and was said to have a view over eight counties. The house was pulled down in 1963 and flats built there.

The Old Well, Banstead.

The Well was an important part of village life until the arrival of piped water. There were many private wells but this was the public one. Around 1895 a severe frost resulted in all the pumps and pipes from Sutton freezing up so water was brought in a cart and sold for 6d a bucket. This was one of the last times the well was used, it was almost 300 feet deep. The 18th century wellhead cover which still houses the elaborate winding gear is a listed building. This view is looking down Park Road; Chucks Meadow was on the right and Yewlands Lodge just behind.

The Chucks, Banstead.

W.T.Brown
The Stationer
Banstead.

Chucks Meadow was a piece of land behind the Woolpack stretching from the Cricket Field to Park Road. The name was probably over 600 years old; in 1369 John Chuck owned land in Banstead. The path in the old postcard goes from Park Road to Avenue Road. The Community Association obtained the meadow as the site for their hall in 1964 but the new building was not opened until 1975 after ten years of fund raising.

YEWLANDS, BANSTEAD.

Yewlands was built around 1730 across the road from Rooks Nest. The Aubertin family lived here for at least 70 years until 1870. In later years the Aubertin sisters ran a girls school. From the turn of the century until the 1930s Mr. Robertson Rodgers J.P. lived here. The house was then demolished and a new housing estate begun in 1938.

Well Farm in Woodmansterne Lane, a timber framed house, is one of the oldest buildings in Banstead being in part over 500 years old. One of the owners, Bishop Sherborne, forged a papal bull to obtain the bishopric of St. David's. Nevertheless he later legitimately became Bishop of Chichester. From 1516 until 1921 it was a working farm owned by a branch of the Lambert family. In 1762 they farmed 500 acres. This picture dated 1914/18 shows the farm buildings and the pond.

The house called Longcroft, now frequented by many people visiting the doctors' surgery, is thought to be 18th century in origin.but with many additions and alterations. From 1860 to 1919 it was owned by John Lambert who rented it out. One tenant was Robert Wigram, a member of the Royal household. At this time the people of Woodmansterne used the Woolpack. When they heard the uproarious noises of a Saturday night the Wigrams used to remark, "There's Woodmansterne going home!". Miss Wigram married in 1921 and the school log notes a very low attendance on the day, perhaps there was a promise of distinguished guests attending. The land in the old picture has now been built on as Fiddicroft and Longcroft Avenues, hence the new photograph shows Longcroft from the front.

Called Rooks Nest when built in 1770, this house was similar in style and appearance to Yewlands across the road. The frontage was later considerably extended and the front door moved. The earliest known occupant was Simon Wilmot but it soon passed to the Lambert family who eventually rented it out. In 1903 it was purchased by Mr. A. Browning to house his preparatory school, Rosehill, from Tunbridge Wells, hence a name change. The school moved to Gloucestershire in 1939 and the house has since been used as offices with a further recent name change to Castle House.

Rosehill on the left and Glenthorne on the right were formerly the home farm and coach house of nearby Rooks Nest. They were both demolished in 1987 to make way for a new housing development.

The four 19th century cottages on the right were pulled down in 1962 to make way for three townhouses. Next door is Wilmot (formerly Jireh) Cottage built in 1841. In 1851 it was being used as an Independent Calvinist Chapel. By 1862 the curate, Edward Buckle, lived here and later Henry Knibbs. Recently the house has been sympathetically renovated. Park Cottage comes next, probably early 18th century. Set back is Woodman's Cottage which dates from the late 18th century and may have gained its name from John Woodman who lived here. All three cottages are listed Grade II.

Boys Surgical Home. Banstead.

Surgical Home for Boys,

PARK ROAD, BANSTEAD.

3,000 Eggs Wanted

Egg Week will be held
APRIL 6th to 13th

GIFTS OF EGGS
WILL BE MOST GRATEFULLY RECEIVED
AND ACKNOWLEDGED.

William Pile, Ltd. Printers, 68-50, High Street, Sutton.

In 1935, 2145 eggs were donated in the week; they were all pickled!

Banstead has long been renowned for its healthy air. Aubrey writing in 1675 mentions the wholesome air prescribed by London physicians for their patients. The Boys Surgical Homes were established at the suggestion of one of the Nightingale nurses who felt that good food and healthy air would aid recovery. This house was built in 1895 and called Parkside. In 1935 the home had cared for 198 boys. At Christmas the boys were visited by Capt. Derek McCulloch, Uncle Mac of Children's Hour who lived in Banstead. The house was taken over by the Invalid Children's Aid Association after the war; they made extensive alterations and renamed it Edith Edwards House after a patron. Very recently the house became a nursing home and was renamed Parkside.

These four pretty brick cottages in Park Road are next to Apsley House and were built mid 19th century, probably for farm labourers.

Banstead Place was built in 1790 by John Motteux, a director of the East India Company, member of a notable Huguenot family and uncle to Lord Palmerston. The Motteux family lived here for fifty years. Later owners were John Lambert and Sir Ralph Neville who moved here from Bentley Lodge. He bequeathed the house to the Worshipful Company of Skinners for charitable purposes. In 1974 they handed over administration to the Queen Elizabeth Foundation for the Disabled and it is now a mobility assessment centre.

Although Mint Farm is a 16th century building, the present Mint Public House is not nearly so old. The first mention is in 1871 when Edward Bennett is described as a beer retailer in the Census. The Bennetts were there for sixty years. The weather-boarded cottages in Park Road are older.

These 10 flint cottages in Mint Road were built in two groups of four in the mid 19th century and the centre two were filled in later.

At the end of the row near Park Road were 10 wash-houses belonging to the cottages. Five of these were demolished in 1987 to make way for two new houses, but it looks as though the remaining ones will stay.

This is now a Conservation Area.

SUTTON LANE, BANSTEAD.

Until the mid 1920s, Sutton Lane was truly a lane sunk between grass banks. The signpost points to the "Oaks, Croydon and Carshalton", now Croydon Lane. The Banstead Hospital can be seen in the distance.

Heath House was built in 1872/5 for Mr. Maynard Taylor. It can just be seen in the far right of the pictures. In 1933 Miss Sabine Pasley opened Greenacre School for Girls here. In 1939 the school was evacuated to Dorset although a few girls stayed in Banstead using the White Cottage. The rest returned in 1944 and the school continues today. The drawing comes from 'The Builder' of 27 October 1888 and shows the new stables and cottage adjoining Heath House.

Banstead Hospital, (originally the Middlesex County Asylum), was built on the site of the Hundred Acres near to the windmill. Opened on 23 March 1877, at its height the hospital accommodated 2500 patients who seem to have had a diet that was dull and not very nutritional. The stone tracks, on the postcard above dated 1915, were laid from Belmont railway station to ease the work of the horse drawn carts bringing building materials, and later supplies of coal to the site. At the time, sheep kept the Downs cropped short. Since they have gone the scrub has grown. The hospital closed in 1987 and at the time of writing its fate is not known.

Banstead. Asylum.

W. Pile Ltd., Sutton

MIDDLESEX COUNTY ASYLUM—BANSTEAD, SURREY
PATIENTS' DIETARY—WEEK COMMENCING 26th MARCH 1877

Day	Breakfast	Dinner	Supper	Vegetables	Ales
Sunday 26	4½ ozs Bread 1 pint Skimmed Milk	Meat & Potato Pie (1 oz Meat per Patient)	6 ozs Bread 1 pint Skimmed Milk	No Vegetables to be issued except Special Diets	There will be 3 pints of Ales given to
Monday 27	4½ ozs Bread Gruel	Vegetable Soup Suet Pudding	6 ozs Bread 1 pint Skimmed Milk	who may have a Chop, Egg or 1 oz Butter as prescribed	each Patient Daily
Tuesday 28	4½ ozs Bread Porridge	Meat & Potato Pie (1 oz Meat per Patient)	6 ozs Bread 1 pint Skimmed Milk	by the Apothecary	
Wednesday 29	4½ ozs Bread 1 pint Skimmed Milk	1½ ozs Meat per Patient (not roasted) Gruel	6 ozs Bread 1 pint Skimmed Milk		
Thursday 30	4½ ozs Bread Gruel	Meat & Potato Pie (1 oz Meat per Patient)	6 ozs Bread 1 pint Skimmed Milk		
Friday 31	4½ ozs Bread Porridge	1½ ozs Meat per Patient (not roasted) Gruel	6 ozs Bread 1 pint Skimmed Milk		
Saturday 1 April	4½ ozs Bread 1 pint Skimmed Milk	Vegetable Soup Suet Pudding	6 ozs Bread 1 pint Skimmed Milk		

By Order of the MEDICAL SUPERINTENDENT
T. CLAYE SHAW, M.D., F.R.C.P.

BOULTERS LANE, BANSTEAD.

Banstead Hall (top right) was built about 1880 and shortly afterwards was bought by the Maitlands. They ran it as a boys preparatory school until 1936 when it was bought by Surrey County Council for an Approved School. To the south was the 'Larches'. Early this century Henry Lambert lived here. It was later run as a girls school by Miss Molyneaux; from 1933 to 1962 it was Aberdour School. Both houses have now been demolished and new housing is under construction. The old houses were approached from the Brighton Road but the volume of traffic has resulted in a new entrance being made from Bolters Lane. The old flint wall remains on the right hand side of the lane. Boulter was an alternative spelling sometimes used.

A large house called Greenhayes stood back from Bolters Lane about where Greenhayes Gardens are now. It was the home of Sir Allen Sarle, Secretary of the London, Brighton & South Coast Railway, until his death in 1903. He had previously lived across Bolters Lane in Bentley Lodge. Later the house was the home of Mr. Trollope. Greenhayes Avenue was built from 1934, part of the widespread development of Banstead at this period.

Wilmot Way, named after one of Banstead's old families, was laid out in 1928. It was one of the first pieces of the Buff House estate to be sold. In the top picture Winkworth Road has not been built. This took place in 1931/2 and was at first called the Banstead by-pass. It took a great deal of traffic away from the High Street.

WILMOT WAY
BANSTEAD.

This postcard, dated 1913, shows that Avenue Road has changed little in 80 years; its future is not so assured at the time of writing. Fern and Laurel Cottages on the left have the Lambert crest on the gable and were built mid 19th century. The development in the High Street and the bank can be seen. The land on the right was Town Field. It was donated to the village in 1925 by Miss Edith Neville as a lasting memorial to her mother, still much enjoyed by Banstead's young and old to this day.

The buildings of Court Farm, one of the oldest farms in Banstead, can just be seen on the extreme right. The cottages in the distance remain but the farm has been replaced by Courtlands Crescent. Opposite the houses and lime trees look remarkably similar today to when they were photographed at the time of the first World War. They had been built ten years previously.

CRICKET BAT MANUFACTURERS,
WHOLESALE AND RETAIL.

Nov 12ᵗʰ 188 9

Banstead C C

Bought of ODD & SON,

55, NORTH END, CROYDON.

Cricket, Lawn Tennis, and Football Materials and Requisites.

IN-DOOR ᴬᴺᴰ OUTDOOR GAMES, ATHLETIC SPORTS OF EVERY DESCRIPTION.

POST OFFICE ORDERS TO BE
MADE PAYABLE AT THE CROYDON
POST OFFICE.

REPAIRS OF ALL KINDS
RECEIVE PROMPT ATTENTION.

ODD'S PATENT FLEXIBLE BAT, PLEASANT TO HANDLE, FREE FROM JAR, AND GREAT DRIVING POWERS.

		£	s	d
May 17ᵗʰ	½ doz Duke Balls @ 5/6	1	13	0
" "	2 sets Bails Ebony & Ash		2	0
" "	2 match Bats @ 12/6	1	5	0
" "	2 Practice Bats 7/6 6/-		13	6
" "	1 pr Gauntlets		8	6
" "	2 prs Batt Gloves @ 5/		10	0
		£4	12	0

Cricket Field, Banstead.

The earliest record of the Cricket Club is of a home match against Twickenham in 1842. Tents and sheds were used for fifty years until a pavilion was built, and another eighty years passed before a second one was erected. The ladies, in 1898, no doubt being tired of sitting without shelter, donated this marquee and 25 chairs. It was not until 1919 that they were allowed into the pavilion – and then only to make the tea and to wash up! Tom Gilbert, landlord of the Victoria, was related to W.G. (Gilbert) Grace the famous cricketer, and he was instrumental in getting Grace to play at Banstead.

These pictures are taken from Garratts Lane, looking across to Court Road. The gate to the left of the original signpost leads to Court House now occupied by St. Ann's School, whilst the other partly visible is the entrance to Garratts Hall. The East Lodge, now a private house, still stands on this corner.

A Charming Bit of Banstead.

W.T. Brown
The Stationer
Banstead.

This pair of semi-detached houses in Bolters Lane was built in 1905. During the 1930s, C. Marland lived in No. 2 'Cleve Cottage', and Mrs. L.E. Spencer in No. 4 which had a large garden. They were replaced by Clifton Place which was first occupied in late 1969.

Holly Lane, Banstead.

The top picture (opposite) shows Park Farm Cottage, originally a lodge to Park House which was demolished in the 1950s. Holly Lane is in the foreground. There are two round storage barns, constructed to exclude the frost pockets which can occur in the corners of rectangular barns. The stable block (bottom right) is surmounted by a clock tower and compass point weather vane. The clock has a dead-beat escapement which is contemporary with the 18th century farm buildings. They are all listed Grade II. No old pictures are known of this farm.

Holly Lane retains its leafy appearance.

67

The Banstead Cure

Shadwell Child: I've had such a lovely dream, it was all about getting well in a country Hospital.
Nurse: Yes, Dear—and we are all trying to make it come true.

(*By kind permission of the Proprietors of "Punch"*)

RÉSUMÉ OF COSTS

NOTE.—The following costs inevitably vary with the fluctuating price of materials, but the donor of any of the undermentioned sums will be entitled to name in perpetuity the unit cited

Hospital	£120,000
Nurses' Home	£42,000
Convalescent Home	£30,000
Single Bed in Hospital	£250
Nurses' Room	£270
Unit of 30 beds, with ward kitchen, examination and bathrooms	£14,000
Infants' Unit of 20 beds	£9,000
Paying Patients' Unit, 15 beds	£7,500
Operating Theatre	£12,500
Laboratories	£3,800
Radiological Department	£3,000

Banstead Wood was designed by R. Norman Shaw in 1884-90 for the Hon. Sir Francis Baring of the banking family. Later it was occupied by the Gartons. In 1936 Queen Elizabeth, now the Queen Mother, laid the foundation stone marking the conversion of the house into a hospital in the country for sick children where they might benefit from the fresh air as an aid to recovery. The schedule of costs on the left comes from the prospectus for the hospital issued in 1934. The right hand part of the original building burnt down in 1938 and has been rebuilt. The hospital was finally opened in 1948. It is still called the Queen Elizabeth Hospital but is now attached to the Manor Hospital, Epsom, and is no longer for children. This is a Grade II listed building.

Garratts Lane was once the main thoroughfare into the village from the Brighton Road; present residents may be forgiven for thinking it still is! Garratts Hall stood behind the wall on the right, well back from the road. In the late 19th century it was the home of John Lambert whose name is mentioned many times in this book as he owned a large amount of property in the village. The Hall was demolished in 1933. Little Garratts can just be seen behind the gates in the new picture. In 1851 it was the farmhouse of Jasper Shallcrass. It is now a private house. The land on the left was also a part of the Garratts Hall estate. It was sold to the Garton family in 1928 and a recreation ground was created. Land fronting the road was sold as building plots in 1938.

Garratts Lane, Banstead.

This picture of Garratts Lane is looking towards Brighton Road. The Victorian row, called Devonshire Cottages, was replaced by Shrubland Court in 1958. In the old view the tiny gap between the fence and the houses was Shrubland Road. Behind the fence the West Lodge of Garratts Hall remains.

Dicelands Road, Banstead.

S.&W. Series   SHRUBLAND ROAD, BANSTEAD.

The picture (top left) is Shrubland Road looking towards Garratts Lane. This was the first part of the road to be built. The postcard is dated 1906 and Mr. Greatley's shop is on the corner of Diceland Road. His sign reads, 'Grocer & Draper: Crowley's Croydon Ales & Stouts'. The centre view looks much the same now as then. Shrubland Road as shown below was not extended to join Lyme Regis Road until after 1945 and the fence in the picture of the fair marked the southern end. Edwards Fair came every year from 1921 until 1938/39.

This view of Diceland Road was taken about 1914 just after the road was extended to the Brighton Road. At first only the part near Shrubland Road was built, then plots were laid out on land belonging to the Gables; the 'kink' in the road marks the join. The London suburbs have many of these smaller Edwardian houses; Banstead has very few and many small businesses were quickly established here. The Burgh Heath telephone exchange was opened around 1923, prior to this it was at Burgh Heath.

The first part of Ferndale Road, adjoining Shrubland Road, was built about the turn of the century, and once again the 'kink' marks the start of the extension to Brighton Road around 1910. The gate on the right has a sign saying 'Cranleigh'. This was the home for twenty years of Edward Gale, village schoolmaster, chairman of Banstead U.D.C. and the first headmaster of the school in Picquets Way. Around 1915 Edgar Pushman became grocer and sub-postmaster and he published many of the postcards used in this book.

Pound Road takes its name from the Pound where stray animals were kept until they were collected. On the 1866 map the Pound is shown as being by the Brighton Road, south of the Council House site. The cottages on the right of the picture date from the middle 1800s, those on the left are later, around 1890. In this book reference has only been made to the pictures on the postcards but the messages on the reverse tell a story too. This delightful one is from Florrie to her Mum in Kentish Town dated 1915. She is evidently staying in a cottage here, "X" marks the spot. Florrie describes the cottage as having a large garden full of flowers and 60 chickens. She promises to bring home flowers and mushrooms and asks, "Can I stay another week Mum?"!

The Lodge, Banstead, Surrey.

This large building began life as a farmhouse in the 1860s. By 1890 it had been enlarged and was called the Lodge, the home of Harrington Hudson JP. In 1898 Miss Mason purchased it and opened a finishing school for young ladies. The newly formed Banstead Urban District Council then bought it in 1933 for the Council House. The gatepost in Chipstead Road still has the name the Lodge.

The Wheatsheaf Inn was originally the Black Boy beerhouse. By 1851 Robert Shallcrass was the landlord. In 1938 the new Wheatsheaf was built directly behind the old one and for a time they stood together. Beyond the pub was Greatley's Highfield Garage, the forerunner of Tanns.

The large signpost points to Garratts Lane, the smaller one opposite is to Great Burgh and Epsom. This would have been along the drive to Nork House, then Church lane and Yew Tree Bottom Road. D.M. Ross, builder, originally had a yard in Diceland Road. The business became Downs Estates and the large advertising board marks their offices at the white house, seen in the picture below. They were one of the developers of the Nork Park estate.

Nork Park Gates.

The gates at the end of the driveway to Nork House bore the inscription 'Omnia Vincit Labor' – work conquers all. In the 1930s they were removed to Kingswood Grange and have since been sold. The side pedestrian gate was always kept open to allow people to use the footpath to Warren Farm.

The Drive was the driveway to Nork House. The view is looking from the Brighton Road. In the extreme right in the old picture is the signpost for the path to Warren Farm and Drift Bridge; you can still walk this footpath. The turning on the right of the new photograph is Woodgavil. This road takes its name from the old manorial rent in which tenants had to cart wood for the Lord of the Manor.

82

Only a few stones, bricks and a mound of earth mark the remains in Nork Park of Nork House. Built in 1740 by Sir Christopher Buckle, the house underwent considerable alteration by later owners, the 6th and 7th Earls of Egmont and Mr. & Mrs. Colman. This view was taken in 1925. But we can still sit on the bench and enjoy the panoramic views over the Thames Valley which attracted Sir Christopher to the site.

This view of Yew Tree Bottom Road was taken from near the road junction on Epsom Downs known as Buckles Gap looking towards Reigate Road. The yew tree, on the left in the 1908 picture, was cut down in 1960 when the Rose Bushes estate was developed.

THE HALDEN ESTATES CO. LTD: N7

Hard to place? This is Nork Way taken in 1927 when much of the area was open parkland, Burgh Wood is in the background. The photograph was taken from about where Park Wood View now is. The house in the centre was built to the plan shown. Halden Estates bought the land from Mrs. Colman of Nork House in 1926. They marked out large plots on which they specified only detached houses could be built. After the company went bankrupt in 1929 the development was continued by Downs Estates and Perry's of Ealing.

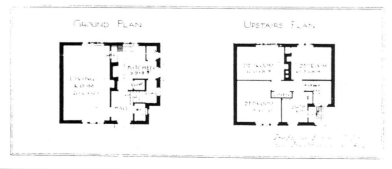

GROUND PLAN   UPSTAIRS PLAN

In medieval times rabbit meat was considered a delicacy and rabbits were 'farmed'. This farm takes its name from the rabbit warren that was here, on land owned by the Buckle family. From about 1730 the sheepwalks were enclosed and the land ploughed up. The drawing is dated 1862. The Driftway is on the site of the farm buildings. The barn at Warren Farm was the earliest social centre in Nork as the new estate developed. Later entertainments were at the Drift Bridge Hotel and it was not until 1963 that the Community Centre was built in Nork Way.

These pictures show the changes in the earliest part of Nork Way. The view above is looking from the shops towards Warren Road on the right. The view (top right) is looking the other way; Eastgate and the shops have replaced the open fields. It was taken before the roads were made-in 1927 Nork Way looked like a quagmire. The picture (middle right) is a little later, still no street lights but the roadside trees are planted. They are mature in the new photographs and make Nork Way attractive in the spring and summer. The white house on the corner of Warren Road has long been a doctor's surgery. Potter & Caiger were physicians and surgeons there in 1934.

The first mention of Tumble Beacon was in 1594 when Mr. Merland was paid for his men watching the beacon. Its elevation would have made it visible for miles and this was just after the threat of invasion from the Spanish Armada. The beacon was originally a Neolithic burial barrow, one of several in the district. It serves as a reminder of our distant ancestors; man has lived hereabouts for thousands of years. The beacon is scheduled as an Ancient Monument and is now in a garden in the Drive.

This picture of Beacon School was taken in 1934 shortly after it was founded by Miss Batts. The little girl was Margaret Burleton on her first day at school. The school was there for 40 years.

The Drift Bridge, Banstead.

PUBLISHED BY
THE SURREY LIBRARY, BANSTEAD.

Looking from the Ewell side of the Drift Bridge towards Banstead this 60 foot arch was the widest span brick-built railway bridge in Surrey when constructed in 1864. The name 'drift' derives from the drovers who used to drive animals to market along the Reigate Road. In wartime the railway was fortified and the tank traps and pill box can be seen by the embankment. The pillar box like structure on the left was an electricity distribution pillar.

The sign next to the garage says 'This site reserved for the Drift Bridge Hotel' which was built in 1932/3. The Fir Tree Tea Shop was popular with both visitors and residents. At the time only two of the present parade of shops had been built but others quickly followed to serve the growing number of residents.

92

The High Beeches estate is built on land that was once the Kensington, Chelsea & St. Marlyebone School for pauper children, later known as Beech-holme. The main gate was in Fir Tree Road but all that remains is one metal upright in the centre of the picture top right. The school was built on the cottage home principle and had nine houses for boys and fourteen for girls, together with a chapel, infirmary, school, workshops, swimming baths and a gymnasium. For forty years there was nothing between the school and Nork House except for Warren Farm. An avenue of beech trees lined the central drive of the school, the same ones which line High Beeches today. The aerial view shows how large an establishment this was, served by its own railway siding. The school was closed in 1975.

Banstead railway station opened on 22 May 1865. The line was built to serve the racing fraternity and at first there were only eight trains a day except race days. The village was a mile away uphill and sparsely populated at the time. Only a few commuters used the line but one of these was Allen Sarle, Secretary of the railway company.

In 1898 the name was changed to Banstead and Burgh Heath and this was to last for thirty years. The name was painted in large letters on the roof to enable pilots to check their course into Croydon Airport. The freight sidings were laid out in 1880, mainly for coal, hence Reckitt and Smith, coal merchants. A regular goods service operated between 1925 and 1935 bringing materials for the house building boom. The line was electrified in 1928 and the station building modernised and extended in 1935 as the commuter traffic built up. For thirty three years Walter Henry Iles was station master. This picture was taken in 1906, outside is Mr. F. Kempsell, his wife-to-be Miss Millicent Marsden and her sister Gladys.

The Brighton Road/Fir Tree Road crossroads had slightly less traffic in 1933 than it does today! In one 24 hours in 1986 over 40,000 cars passed along Brighton Road, as well as 15,000 on Fir Tree Road and 22,000 on Winkworth Road. This picture is taken from Fir Tree Road looking to Winkworth Road. The traffic lights were installed in 1936. Improvements to the A217 began in 1939 but wartime intervened and the first dual-carriageway section was not completed until 1962.

The school playground is now part of the site of the Waitrose supermarket.

As foreshadowed on page 21 a new school was built in the Horseshoe and the site of the 1858 village school became a supermarket in 1990.

The new picture is taken from the same view point as that on page 20.

The new housing development is now called "Rosehill Farm Meadow"

The Banstead Hospital was substantially demolished and replaced by the Downview and Highdown prisons. The picture shows the present entrance.

Fern and Laurel Cottages and the former schoolmaster's househave been replaced by the supermarket car park. The school warning sign remains!

The Pavilion in the Lady Neville recreation ground, opened in 1939, was burnt down by vandals and has been replaced by a modern version.

The top picture shows the main block of St. Anne's R. C. School (formerly Court Farm) which was re-developed in 1998, with new outbuildings.

INDEX

Aberdour School	56
All Saints Church	8, 9, 11
Apsley Cottages	48
Avenue Road	21, 60
Bank	22, 31, 34
Banstead Hall	56
Banstead Hospital	52, 54
Banstead Place	49
Banstead Wood	69
Baring family	69
Beacon School	89
Beacon Way	89
Beech-holme	93
Black Boy Beerhouse	78
Bolters Lane	56, 65
Boys Surgical Home	47
Brew's Garage	14
Brighton Road	78, 79, 95
Buckle family	8, 10, 46, 82, 85
Buckles Gap	83
Buff Avenue	27
Buff House	15, 24, 27, 36, 58
Burgh Wood	84
Chucks Meadow	39, 40
Church Institute	12, 13
Clifton Place	65
Community Association Hall	40
Council House	77
Court Farm	61
Court Road	61, 64
Courtlands Crescent	61
Cricket Club	62
Croydon Lane	52
Diceland Road	73, 74
Downs Estates	79, 84
Downview Prison	54a
Drift Bridge	90
Drift Bridge Hotel	85, 91
The Driftway	85
The Drive	81, 88
Edith Edwards' House	47
Ferndale Road	75
Fiddicroft Avenue	43
Fir Tree Road	91, 92, 93, 95
The Forge	33
French & Foxwell	14, 26
Gale, Edward	75
Garton family	69, 70
Garratts Hall	70
Garratts Lane	10, 64, 70, 71, 79
Glenthorne	45
Greenacre	53
Greenhayes Avenue	7, 58
Halden Estates	84
Heath House	53
High Beeches	93
Highfield Garage	79
High Street	6–37
Holly Lane	64, 66
Ivy House	26, 29
Knibbs, Henry	8, 19, 46
Lady Neville Rec. Ground	60
Lambert family	8, 19, 24, 30, 38, 42, 43, 44, 49, 60, 70
The Larches	57
Little Garratts	70
Longcroft	43
Longcroft Avenue	43
The Lodge	77
Mint Cottages	51
Mint Farm	50
Mint Public House	50
Neville family	49, 60
Nork Community Centre	85
Nork House	80, 81, 82, 84, 93
Nork Park	82, 84
Nork Way	84, 86
Park Cottage	46
Park Farm	66
Park Road	38–51
Police station	25, 26
Post Office	10, 29
Pound Road	76
Pushman, Edgar	75
QEFD (Mobility Centre)	49
Queen Elizabeth Hospital	69
Railway station	94
Rooks Nest	44
Rosehill	44
Rosehill farmhouse	45
St. Anne's School	61a
Salisbury Road	36
Shrubland Road	71, 73
Sutton Lane	31, 37, 52
Tonges	29
Town Field	60
Tumble Beacon	88
Vicarage	10
Victoria Hotel	6
Village school	17–21
War Memorial	35
Warren Farm	85, 93
Watkin's Garage	15
The Well	39
Well Farm	9, 30, 42
Well House	31, 38
The Wheatsheaf	78
Wilmot Cottage	46
Wilmot Way	7, 59
Winkworth Cottage	7
Winkworth Road	58, 95
Woodgavil	81
Woodman's Cottage	46
Woodmansterne Lane	39, 42
The Woolpack	30, 31, 34
Yewlands	39, 41
Yew Tree Bottom Road	83